Field Work Savvy

A Handbook for Students
in Internship,
Co-Operative Education,
Service-Learning and
other forms of
Experiential Education

Field Work Savvy

A Handbook for Students
in Internship,
Co-Operative Education,
Service-Learning and
other forms of
Experiential Education

JOAN MILNES

A Division of WINEPRESS PUBLISHING

Packaged by WinePress Publishing, PO Box 428, Enumclaw, WA 98022. The views expressed or implied in this work do not necessarily reflect those of WinePress Publishing. The author(s) is ultimately responsible for the design, content and editorial accuracy of this work.

Unless otherwise noted, all Scriptures are taken from the Holy Bible, New International Version, Copyright © 1973, 1978, 1984 by the International Bible Society. Used by permission of Zondervan Publishing House. The "NIV" and "New International Version" trademarks are registered in the United States Patent and Trademark Office by International Bible Society.

Scripture references marked KJV are taken from the King James Version of the Bible.

Scripture references marked NASB are taken from the New American Standard Bible, © 1960, 1963, 1968, 1971, 1972, 1973, 1975, 1977 by The Lockman Foundation. Used by permission.

ISBN 1-57921-571-8
Library of Congress Catalog Card Number: 2002117871

Dedication

To Jamie Jamieson,
good friend and erstwhile editor

Proceeds from the sale of this book will serve the needy.

Share with God's people who are in need.
Romans 12:13

There will always be poor people in the land. Therefore I command you to be openhanded toward your brothers and toward the poor and needy in your land.
Deuteronomy 15:11

Table of Contents

Acknowledgements

Ellen Wicklum, Editor, University Press of New England and John H. Quigley, Professor of Sociology, Salem (MA) State College
- for providing enlightenment, encouragement and confidence.

The National Society for Experiential Education
- for supporting this book and providing professional organization and forum for its dedicated membership.

My mother, Adele Elgosin, of Millers Falls, MA
- for being my biggest cheerleader.

My husband Bradford Milnes and our children Thomas Milnes and Donna Milnes
- for the blessings they are to me.

Introduction for Students

Congratulations! You are reading this book because you are a student preparing to participate in field work. You are about to embark on the adventure that John Dewey (the father of educational philosophy) called, "the organic connection between education and personal experience."

In other words . . . you will be learning by doing.

In other words still . . . experience is the best teacher.

Field work takes several forms—internship, cooperative education, service-learning, school-to-work, externship, clinical and teacher practica, and adventure learning. Some of these forms of field work are associated with specific occupations like those in the medical field (clinical practicum) and teaching (teacher practicum). Others refer to a specific purpose like community service (service-learning), physical challenge (adventure learning), facilitating the transition from student to employee (school-to-work), and earning money (co-operative education). All of these forms of non-classroom learning are broadly defined as field work or experiential education.

Field Work Savvy is a handbook for students in college, high school and graduate school. The type of field work or experiential education program and its requirements vary by institution and according to the age and ability level of the student, but there is a *process* that is common for all students. This book is a guide through that process, a guide that will take you through all the steps, from landing your field work site to learning from the experience long after it ends, and everything in between.

Field Work Savvy guides you through the steps of

- searching and applying for field work opportunities,
- developing a resume,
- creating a portfolio,
- interviewing,
- determining goals,

- completing the learning contract,
- utilizing best practices during and after field work,
- practicing reflection,
- acquiring letters of recommendation,
- bringing closure to the field work,
- and more!

Sprinkled throughout this book are tips containing advice from experienced students, wisdom from veteran site supervisors, and guidance from field work professionals. This insider information is presented under the headings of

   **Pointer**

and

From the Field

The information following these headings will give you insight into what is probably a first-time experience for you.

Why participate in field work?

Some field work is required, but there are many good reasons to participate as an elective. The prime reason has already been mentioned—experience is the best teacher. Much is learned in the classroom setting, but to integrate academics with the world of work and to make the transition from academia to employment, there is no better vehicle than field work.

Additionally, while you are gaining skills and knowledge through hands-on practice and observation of others in the workplace, you are also making contacts in the field, gaining valuable resume-building experience and developing portfolio material, elements that will be important for future job-hunting. You are also focusing your career, a vision that normally can be a little fuzzy for students. Field work helps you discover what you like and, equally important, what you don't like. Last, but certainly not least, field work promotes personal growth, interpersonal skills and self-confidence.

An Historic Perspective

Exposing youth to the work environment is not a new idea. Consider the past practices of apprenticeships and indentured service. The definitions of these words ring with the meaning of field work. Webster's Unabridged Dictionary gives both temporal and practical meanings for apprenticeship:

- "The term for which an apprentice serves"
- "Preliminary practice or training."

Indenture bears similar meaning:

- "A contract binding one person to work for another for a given length of time, as an apprentice to a master."

Webster further defines indenture this way:

- "In law, a written agreement between two or more parties. Indentures were originally in duplicate, laid together and indented or cut in a waving line, so that the two papers or parchments corresponded to each other."

Analogously, a student who participates in field work learns how behavior in the workplace must be shaped ("indented or cut") to fit ("correspond") with an employer's needs and expectations.

In Summary

Field work, or experiential education, is a type of learning that complements classroom experience.

Each academic institution determines how it is utilized. For example,

- co-operative education (co-op) may be an elective receiving transcript notation, but no grade and no credit,
- service-learning may be a pass/fail, credit-bearing elective,
- internship may be a graded, credit-bearing requirement.

Whatever form experiential education takes at your college, high school or graduate school, your participation in it will broaden your horizons and enhance your learning about the world of work and about yourself.

Field Work Savvy shows you how to make the most of your field experience. Using this book as your guide, you will be able to approach and proceed through the experience with confidence and enthusiasm about your opportunity to make "the organic connection between education and personal experience."

Introduction for Experiential Educators

As you know, students approach field work with varying degrees of anxiety and enthusiasm. Generally speaking, a more confident and eager individual is attracted to elective field work compared to the broad range of attitudes expressed by students who are required to participate.

Apprehension about participating in an experiential education program is a reflection of the student feeling unsure, unskilled, unwanted, inexperienced, or a potential burden to the sponsor. These feelings are natural and are addressed as part of preparing the student to enter the field.

Several sections in Chapter 1 are useful when working with hesitant students.

- "Addressing Fears & Anxieties" acknowledges the worries students experience about field work.
- "Reasons Employers Welcome Students" describes why employers want students in the workplace.
- A discussion of the Socratic Method reveals the benevolent attitude of the site supervisor.
- "Search Methods" tells how to find field work opportunities.

Information contained in these sections will boost student confidence. As a result, energy that might have been spent on fretting will become available for learning in the field.

Additionally, *Field Work Savvy* provides three useful lists:

- Motivations for employers to sponsor students participating in field work (helpful for promoting field work to employers as well as when counseling anxious students),
- Benefits experiential education programs bring to institutions of learning (helpful for promoting field work within academic institutions), and

- Tips for site supervisors (helpful for guiding mentors).

Experiential educators frequently encounter opportunities to utilize these lists when working with the various parties to field work.

Finally, sample documents in this book are intended to give students a basic acquaintance with some of the paperwork involved with field work. Each institution will have its own version of the learning contract. Resumes are a reflection of individual style or pre-formatted templates.

The blank sample documents are intended to assist students in organizing their thoughts and information. Students are encouraged to use them as preliminary worksheets and to practice developing their own goals in the goal-writing framework provided in Chapter 4.

Introduction for Faculty and Administrators

Acollege dean once described field work administrators by making a Biblical allusion to their professional position. He referred to experiential educators as being "in this world, but not of this world," (John 17:11,14). The dean was not implying any supernatural ability to walk on water or perform miracles. Instead, he was describing the fact that experiential educators work in the world of academia but are not academics. For this reason, proponents of field work sometimes encounter resistance within institutions of learning.

Academic institutions embrace experiential education to varying degrees. Some incorporate field work into the curriculum, sometimes making it a requirement. When required, experiential education becomes systemic. Administration, faculty, advisors, staff, students and parents accept the notion and promote the concept of field experience.

On the other hand, some institutions of learning are less accepting of non-traditional education. Some faculty and administrators view experience outside the classroom as non-academic and therefore not worthy of credit or transcript notation. This philosophy denies the student an avenue for learning and the opportunity to gain practical experience.

This philosophy also denies the academic institution opportunities to expand public relations and boost placement statistics for guidance and career services. Consider the benefits enjoyed by academic institutions that maintain experiential education programs.

Benefits for Academic Institutions with Experiential Education Programs

Benefit #1:   It's good PR. Students participating in field work promote an institution to the community. Plus, opportunities can be created to provide community service.

Benefit #2:   Experiential education programs provide another avenue of learning.

Learning is what academic institutions are about. Providing opportunities for field work expands offerings and keeps them in line with the educational purpose.

Benefit #3:   Experiential education programs broaden horizons within the academic community. Students with field experience bring to campus new ideas and fresh perspectives that stimulate discussion inside and outside the classroom.

Benefit #4:   Experiential education programs provide a boost to placement statistics for career services and guidance departments. Many students are offered entry-level positions with their field work sponsors while some sponsors convert field work students to full-time employees. New hires in general often have some field experience, even when that experience was acquired elsewhere.

Benefit #5:   The boost to job placement statistics described in Benefit #4 increases the reputation and desirability of the institution to prospective students. This can drive up the number of applicants to the institution.

Benefit #6: Secondary schools, colleges and graduate schools enjoy increased visibility as their students participate in field work in the local area, in the nation, and in the world.

Benefit #7: Research institutions stay on the cutting edge by using experiential education programs as a direct link to learning what is needed by business, industry and science, then focusing institutional resources on those needs.

Simply stated, by including field work opportunities in its offerings, an academic institution reaps many benefits for itself and for its students.

Chapter 1

Getting Started

Some students reading this book will be placed into field work sites by the college or school; other students will be responsible for finding and choosing their own sites. For students taking an active role in the search, you must first decide *what* you want to do and *where* you want to do it.

What you want to do is dependent upon your interests. You will want something that relates to your field of study or to your favorite classes or to something you are interested in exploring.

Where you participate in field work is usually determined by where you live or where you attend school, or where you can stay with a friend or relative.

For most students, these are fairly straightforward issues. Your next step will be to research your options. For students unsure of what to do for field work, please see "Getting Started Tip #6" at the end of this chapter.

Many resources are available to help you zero in on the best site for you. The next sections of this chapter discuss those resources and describe how to make contact with sites.

RESOURCES FOR RESEARCHING YOUR OPTIONS

Your College, High School or Graduate School
The career center or guidance office probably has a database of field work sites previously held by students as well as leads on other opportunities. An experiential education professional is usually available to provide some level of assistance in your search. As already stated, some institutions match you to or place you into a site. Other institutions hold the philosophy that the process of being involved with finding your field work is good preparation for the job search.

As part of managing a field work program, experiential education professionals work to establish new partnerships and to maintain good relationships with existing ones. Experiential educators hold titles like Co-Operative Education Specialist, Service-Learning Coordinator, Director of Internships, and School-to-Work Counselor. In some academic institutions, they may provide services from an experiential education office, or they may work as part of a team in the guidance department or the career center, or they may be faculty members within academic departments. Whatever their status is at your high school, college or graduate school, they will be your partners and best resource for researching your options and completing a successful field experience.

Family & Friends

Tell people you are looking for field work. People who know you may be aware of opportunities and recommend you to specific sites. Contacts are made this way.

Reference Books

References books listing specific field work opportunities, names of contacts and how to apply in the US and abroad can be found in libraries and bookstores. Check with your career center or guidance office, too.

Yellow Pages

A handy resource for researching potential sites is the Yellow Pages. Let's say you are interested in working with animals. Look up animal hospitals, animal shelters, zoos, and veterinarians. Plan to contact all listings in locations where you are willing to travel or that are accessible by public transportation. If you do not have a hard copy of the Yellow Pages for the geographical area in which you are interested, go to www.YellowPages.com on the Internet.

World Wide Web

Although students seeking internship opportunities on the World Wide Web will find more information than students seeking other forms of field work, the Internet is not a best resource for any form of field work. A better use of the Internet is for researching specific companies and organizations by visiting their Web sites and by visiting your college or school field work Web pages.

For students who are seeking internships and who wish to see what opportunities can be found on the Internet, use a search engine by typing in the word *internships* along with qualifiers like career field or geographic location. For example:

professional sports marketing internships
or
graphic design internships boston

Many Web sites are devoted to internships; others have links to information about internships. Some popular Web addresses include:

www.coolworks.com
www.internabroad.com
www.internjobs.com
www.internship4america.com
www.internshipprograms.com
www.internships.com
www.internshipsforstudents.com
www.internweb.com
www.jobweb.com
www.petersons.com
www.rsinternships.com
www.usinterns.com
www.wetfeet.com

Established partnerships between academic institutions and employers for service-learning, co-op, school-to-work, externship and internship will not be found via an Internet search, although they may be posted on your school or college Web pages. Additionally, clinical rotations and teaching practica take place in fields that require professional certification and must be completed at sites approved by the appropriate governing agency. Adventure learning offers pre-established programs of physical challenge and self-discovery that usually do not involve an employer. For these reasons, your experiential education professional will be a better resource for you than the World Wide Web.

MAKING CONTACT

Your research should yield a few places of interest to you. The next step is contacting those places to learn about availability and opportunity. There are several ways to do this.

Telephone Calls

Introduce yourself and explain why you are calling. If you do not have a contact, ask for the name of the person with whom you should speak about doing field work there. What you say should sound something like this:

> "Hi. My name is Stephen Student. I attend Knowledge College. Can you tell me who I should talk to about doing a co-op at [the name of the place you're calling]?"

Have a notepad ready. Ask for the spelling of the person's name. Take notes and jot down questions you want to ask. Plan to call several places because not all sites will take students or have openings.

Letters of Inquiry

Another way to make contact with a site is by sending a letter of inquiry. The letter should introduce yourself, state where you are a student, what you are studying, and the type of field work you are seeking. The letter should be addressed to the person at the site who can respond to your inquiry. Be sure the name is spelled correctly and the proper title is used. Ask someone to proofread it. You may or may not include a resume with this letter. If you include a resume, refer to it in the body of the letter. Resume writing will be discussed in Chapter 2.

Finally, state in the last paragraph that you will call the person in a few days to discuss the field work. Be sure to call the person two or three days after he or she has received your letter. If you wait too long, the person may have trouble recalling your letter. Also, it will appear that you are not interested enough to follow-up promptly and are therefore not a good risk for the site to accept you for field work. A letter of inquiry should look something like the sample letter on the next page.

Knowledge College
City, State Zip
Date

Name of Contact
Job Title
Name of Employer
Address
City, State Zip

Dear Mr./Ms. Contact Person,

I am a sophomore at Knowledge College studying Finance. I am interested in acquiring an internship with an investment firm to learn more about portfolio management.

My coursework so far has included Introduction to Finance, Accounting, International Marketing and Investment Strategies. I am interested in learning more about investment strategies and portfolio management.

The internship I seek is for three credits and is to last eight weeks beginning anytime after final exams end on May 10. I will appreciate the chance to speak with you and to give you more details about the internship program at Knowledge College.

A copy of my resume is enclosed. I will contact you in a few days to discuss internship opportunities with [Name of Employer]. If you prefer to contact me, I can be reached at telephone #123-456-7890, the address printed above, or at e-mail address stephen.student@knowledge.edu.

Thank you for your time and consideration.

Sincerely,

Stephen Student

E-Mail

Because unexpected and uninvited e-mail can be flagged as spam, some busy people delete these messages without opening them. For this reason, contact a site by e-mail only if you are asked to do so or if the sponsor's Web site makes it an option. If the sponsor does invite you to make contact electronically, be sure all spelling, grammar and punctuation are correct, just as you would with the hard copy of a letter of inquiry.

Unscheduled Visits

Dropping in is another way to make contact. You will be able to see the site and learn the name of, or possibly meet the person responsible for field work students. Also, you can pick up any application materials the sponsor may require. Before making an unscheduled visit, read about first impressions in the *Appearance & Timing* section of Chapter 3.

The rest of this chapter contains six tips about getting started in your field work. Each tip includes an example to illustrate the point.

GETTING STARTED TIP #1

Start early!

By waiting until the last minute, you increase your chances of having to take what you can get, rather than getting what you want. By starting early, you increase your chances of finding more than one field work opportunity from which to choose. This can be helpful before and after the field work begins. Consider Janet's experience.

From the Field

"I wanted a co-op in a fast-paced corporate environment. I started looking way before the deadline and I wore a business suit. I interviewed with about seven different companies. Every company offered me a co-op and each one sounded better than the ones before it. I started thinking it might be a problem deciding which one to take!"

Janet discovered this was not a bad problem to have. Shortly after the field work began at the site she selected, she called her co-op advisor to talk about the amount of guidance she was receiving from her supervisor.

"I had a lot of questions, but my supervisor was very busy and she couldn't stop to answer my questions all the time. So then I started wondering if I should switch my co-op because I still had the offers from those other places. I called my advisor about what to do."

Janet acknowledged that her supervisor was committed to the weekly meetings outlined in her learning contract (Learning Contracts are discussed in Chapter 4) and that she liked the stimulating environment and the challenge of having to figure out work issues for herself. Also, Janet fit the profile of the type of student the company sought - motivated and able to work independently with little supervision.

"My advisor told me to wait a while to see how I felt about it after I'd been there a little longer. I'm glad I did because it all turned out okay. My supervisor was really terrific and she gave me work like everyone else in the marketing and PR department. I had my own desk and computer, too, but I don't think I would have been happy there if I didn't have the other offers. Even though I stayed and it worked out, I would have felt like I *had* to stay if I didn't have the other offers. This way it was my choice."

GETTING STARTED TIP #2

Addressing Fears & Anxieties

Some students become anxious about asking for and completing field work. Thinking they have nothing to offer a sponsor, they feel awkward, out of place, in the way, unwanted, or just plain scared. These are normal feelings. Students frequently feel the way these students felt before starting field work.

From the Field

"I know where I want to do my service-learning, but what if they want someone who can do the work? I don't know much about community access TV or video production."—Jonathan

"I won't know anybody there. Won't they get kinda mad, like they have to baby-sit me?" —Alicia

"I understand what I am supposed to do, but, well, it's just that I'm really nervous. I've never asked for an internship before."—Veronica

Relax!

The reason you participate in field work is to learn about something of interest to you, but with which you have little or no experience. Sponsors know this and want your experience to be successful for you, *and for them.* Because they are employers, sponsors benefit by hosting students. There are several reasons employers embrace field work programs. Understanding these reasons will help you find your sense of place as a student in the world of work.

REASONS EMPLOYERS WELCOME STUDENTS

Reason #1   Sponsors use the field work program as a recruitment tool. The field work program is an opportunity for sponsors (employers) to learn about a student's abilities and work ethic.

Sponsors can observe how the student fits into the workplace and they can train the student in the ways of their work environment.

Reason #2   Students are a low-cost alternative to hiring new or temporary employees. When a student takes over certain tasks, employees are freed up to complete other work and to start new projects. Students can also be useful during employee vacations or when a temp is needed to complete a short-term project.

During a slow economy when companies cut back, field work programs may be maintained and sometimes expanded. This strategy allows employers to continue to bring in workers at a lower cost or at no cost and without the expense of providing benefits. At the same time they continue to develop their talent pool (Reason #1). When the economy rebounds, the employer will know which students will make the best hires.

40

Reason #3   Sponsors welcome students for the "new blood" they bring into the workplace. Students are typically young, enthusiastic and full of energy, optimism and new ideas. Not only do they present a fresh perspective, they can be a catalyst for change by challenging the status quo. They also bring diversity to the workplace, an especially desirable factor in global and international business.

Reason #4   Sponsors may use field work programs to determine whether an employee is management material by assigning that employee as the student's supervisor, then observing the employee's management skills.

Reason #5   Maintaining a field work program builds a relationship with the community in which the employer is located. Field work programs are viewed as community service and promote the sponsor's image. Employers welcome opportunities for positive PR.

Reason #6   By linking themselves through field work programs with education, particularly higher education, employers can communicate their needs and potentially influence changes in curriculum to suit those needs. In this manner employers can shape an even more finely tuned pool of potential employees.

For these reasons, employers welcome students into the workplace. Knowing these reasons will help you enter the workplace with confidence, thus setting the tone to get the most out of your time in the field.

Consider Socrates

Now that you have the *practical* reasons that students are desired in the workplace, let's get *philosophical* for a moment. Socrates, the ancient Greek philosopher, believed that all knowledge is inborn. Further, he believed anyone could learn anything if someone is willing to teach by drawing out the knowledge. This form of teaching is called the Socratic Method. It is not the modern style of formal instruction designed to match teaching styles with learning styles. Rather, it is a form of mentoring that can be utilized successfully by anyone who

1. has knowledge and
2. is willing to share that knowledge.

Implicit in the Socratic Method is the benevolent attitude of the teachers towards the students because the teachers who have the knowledge are *willing* to share that knowledge.

This describes site supervisors as well because

1. they have knowledge of the field and
2. by agreeing to be supervisors, they are willing to share that knowledge.

Therefore, like the teacher-student relationship, the supervisor-student relationship is a benevolent one.

Still have Fears and Anxieties?

If you are still nervous after reading how field work programs benefit sponsors and how supervisors are willing to share their knowledge with students, speak with your field work advisor. Experiential education professionals are familiar with these fears and can help you work through them.

GETTING STARTED TIP #3

Leaving & Receiving Voice Mail

When leaving a voice message, be sure to speak slowly and clearly. Busy people delete messages that are difficult to hear because of rapid or garbled speech. It is helpful to spell your name and to leave your name and phone number twice, once at the beginning of the message and again at the end.

When you know you will be receiving voice messages from potential field work sponsors, be sure your voice mail greeting sounds professional. Eliminate background noise, music and other "entertaining" greetings. State clearly your name or phone number so the caller can be sure he or she has reached *your* voice mail.

From the Field

Here is a sampling of student voice mail greetings that do not make a positive impression and therefore should be avoided.

"Yo! I ain't here. You know what to do." BEEP.
This student does not identify himself and he uses jargon acceptable to his peers, but not to professionals.

Ethereal music lasting a l-o-o-o-o-n-g time then a distant-sounding voice saying, "Hi, this is Rachel. I can't answer the phone right now," and more ethereal music lasting another l-o-o-o-o-n-g time. BEEP.

Making a busy person wait is an invitation to receive a "click!" instead of a message. Also, Rachel sounds like she may be engaging in recreational chemicals.

Loud music. "Leave a message. If you're lucky, I'll call you back." BEEP.

This student does not identify himself and his attitude, while probably meant to be funny, puts callers on the defensive.

GETTING STARTED TIP #4

Follow Directions

Some sponsors are very informal about accepting students for field work. Some rely only on a verbal agreement between the supervisor and the student. Other sponsors have formal application procedures that may involve an interview, filling out forms, providing a resume, supplying proof of student status, etc. Sponsors with formal application procedures include broadcast media, government agencies, sites where security is a factor, and sites that are extremely popular with students.

Carefully follow application instructions, especially when applying for competitive field work opportunities. Failure to follow instructions is the first criteria some sponsors use to cut students from their large applicant pools. Consider this advice from Ms. M, internship coordinator for the aquarium in a large city.

From the Field

"We require all our internship applicants to start the application process online. People who do not specifically follow the directions outlined on our Web site are the first to be cut from the applicant pool. We have to do it this way because we get so many people applying for internships. We have to reduce it to a manageable number."

See Chapters 2 & 3 to learn more about applying for field work opportunities. These chapters discuss interviewing, how to develop a resume, and how to take the unusual step of creating a portfolio if you want to get the edge on the competition!

GETTING STARTED TIP #5

Get with the Program!

Experiential education programs are carefully designed learning opportunities. Some students may not see the big picture or fully understand how it fits in with education. Trust that the program requirements will be beneficial to you. Do not try to bypass parts of the program or look for an easy way out.

From the Field

Doug grew angry upon hearing through the grapevine that two of his classmates had falsified their time sheets. He lodged a complaint with his field work advisor declaring it unfair for them to receive the same credit as he and others who completed the time requirement.

The advisor agreed, if the hearsay was true, that it would be unfair. The advisor also pointed out that Doug and the other students who successfully completed the time requirement earned valuable resume-building experience. They now own what they learned and can use it to advance their careers. Cheating students do not have this long-term advantage. They will come to that realization as the thrill of getting away with something wears off.

Further, be aware that many experiential education programs have policies against participating in field work at sites where relatives work. The wisdom of such a policy ensures objective treatment and evaluation of the student. Plus, future employers will view differently evaluations and letters of recommendation written by relatives and by people who report to relatives.

GETTING STARTED TIP #6

Two Resources for Students Who Don't Know What They Want for Field Work

Informational Interviewing

Some students reading this book are unsure about what type of work to pursue. It may be helpful for you to learn about a specific job and to obtain advice from someone doing that job. This can be accomplished through informational interviewing. Simply contact someone working at a job you wish to explore and explain that you will appreciate the opportunity to ask him or her a few questions. Here are some questions to ask during an information-gathering interview.

- What is a typical day like for you?
- Why did you choose to do this type of work?
- What do you like and dislike about the work?
- What do you need to know and be able to do to be successful?

- What type of education is required?
- Is there high demand for this type of work?
- What advice would you give to someone considering this line of work?
- Who else could I talk with about this type of work?

Notice that all you are asking for is information and advice. Most people enjoy giving information and advice as well as talking about their work.

This is not a time to ask for a field work opportunity. This is a time to gather information and advice. In the process, you might make a contact that leads to a field work opportunity, but that is not the purpose of informational interviewing.

Standardized Testing

Standardized testing can be helpful if you are unsure of what to pursue. Guidance departments and career centers usually provide tests like career assessments or skills and interest inventories. Arrange to take one of these tests to help you find out what you want to do.

Field Work Savvy

CHAPTER 2

Resume & Portfolio

Resumes and portfolios are forms of communication that provide information about you. The first part of this chapter discusses how to develop a resume that will be useful when applying for field work opportunities. The latter part of this chapter discusses how to create a portfolio showcasing you as a student applicant for field work.

THE RESUME

An effective resume is one that communicates relevant information about you and presents that information in a reader-friendly format. This section provides instruction and advice for developing an effective resume. If you want to learn more, there are many books and software that deal with resume-writing. You may wish to review some of them. Search libraries, bookstores and the Internet for materials that teach the basics in clear, simple terms. Also, guidance departments and career centers provide resume-writing materials and assistance.

Keep in mind there is no "correct" way to write a resume and there is no particular format that is "the best." However, some styles of writing and some layout formats are better than others. This chapter will help you decide what information to include in your resume and how to present that information both in writing and in layout to make it reader-friendly.

As a student applying for field work, your resume should be one or two pages long. The length will depend on how much experience you have. Typically, the older the student, the longer the resume will be.

Layout

The resume printed on the next page is an example of one way a resume may be prepared. Notice the format and the writing style. It is easy to look at because it is neat and uncluttered. Information is communicated through phrases that begin with action verbs. In short, it is a reader-friendly document that provides relevant information.

Stephanie Student
Knowledge College
City, State Zip
Telephone
stephanie.student@knowledge.edu

OBJECTIVE

To obtain a service-learning position with a non-profit human services agency where my Web page design skills will be used.

EDUCATION

B.S. [year of anticipated graduation] Computers & Information Technology	Knowledge College City, State
Diploma [year of graduation]	Name of High School City, State

RELEVANT COURSEWORK

Computer Applications	Online Network Exploration
Survey of Computer Science	Web Design & Development

RELATED EXPERIENCE

Volunteer Webmaster, [dates]

My House of Worship

City, State

Edited and maintained Web pages using Front Page.
Updated information provided by committees, clergy
and youth group.

Camp Counselor, Summer [year]

Computer Camp

City, State

Taught school-age children basic and intermediate
computer skills in Word, Power Point and Paint.

OTHER EXPERIENCE

Concession Attendant, December [year]–August [year]

Metro Movie Theater

City, State

Waited on customers. Operated cash register.
Restocked display cases and container dispensers.

COMMUNITY INVOLVEMENT

Participate in annual Family Fun Run 5K Road Race
fundraiser since [year] to support local United Way.

INTERESTS

Running, cycling, music, movies.

REFERENCES

Furnished upon request.

References for Stephanie Student

Name (**Frank Faithful**)
Job Title (**Clergy**)
Place of Employment (**My House of Worship**)
City, State
Telephone Number

Name (**Suzie Software**)
Job Title (**Program Director**)
Place of Employment (**Computer Camp**)
City, State
Telephone Number

Name (**Timothy Technology**)
Job Title (**IT Instructor**)
Place of Employment (**Knowledge College**)
City, State
Telephone Number

Name (**Charity Jones**)
Job Title (**Events Coordinator**)
Place of Employment (**United Way**)
City, State
Telephone Number

Sections of the Resume

Look at Stephanie Student's resume for an example of each section described below.

- The **HEADING** is composed of name, mailing address and phone number. An e-mail address may also be included. Traditionally this information appears at the top of the resume. A variation of this format is to place only the name at the top with the address and phone number running across the bottom of the page. <u>Note</u>: The words "resume," "curriculum vitae" (Latin for "course of life") and "vita" (Latin for "life") should not be used. It is understood that this is a resume; there is no need to label it.

- The **OBJECTIVE** gives the reason for writing the resume. This section expresses what it is you are looking for, which is a specific type of field work.

- **EDUCATION** tells the reader about your academic background. If you have not yet completed secondary school, college or graduate school, this section will tell the reader when you expect to graduate. For college and graduate students it will also tell the reader which degree you are completing.

- **RELEVANT COURSEWORK** tells the reader which courses you have taken that are related to the type of field work you are seeking.

- The section on **EXPERIENCE** can be divided into **RELATED EXPERIENCE** and **OTHER EXPERIENCE**. The former will list volunteer and/or work experience related to the type of field work you seek. The latter lists volunteer and/or work experience unrelated to the type of field work you seek. If you do not need both categories, use **EXPERIENCE** as the title for this section.

- As needed, additional sections may be created to present more information. For example, **COMMUNITY SERVICE** or **INTERESTS** or **SPECIAL SKILLS** or **MILITARY EXPERIENCE** or **AWARDS** or **CERTIFICATION(S)** or **ADDITIONAL TRAINING** are section titles that provide a place on the resume to communicate more about your background.
Note: Do not include personal information such as height, weight, or marital status. This

type of information is not relevant to your interests or your ability to successfully participate in field work.

• **REFERENCES** is always the final section of the resume. Under that title should be the words "Furnished upon request." Never place the names of your references on your resume. Instead, have a separate sheet entitled "References for YOUR NAME" which lists the name, title, address and phone number of three or four people who have agreed *in advance* to provide you with a positive reference in the event a field work sponsor contacts them. References are people who know you and who can speak positively about your skills, work ethic, and/or character. Employers, teachers, and contacts at clubs and volunteer organizations are good choices. Keep a copy of your reference sheet handy so that your references can be "furnished upon request."

Some resume writers place these sections in a different order and label some sections with different words. Except for the **HEADING** and the **OBJECTIVE** which should be the first and second sections, respectively, and **REFERENCES**, which always appears last, you may wish to rearrange the sections. It is a good idea, however, to keep **EDUCATION** and **RELEVANT COURSEWORK** in sequence. If you have two sections of **EXPERIENCE**, they too should be placed in sequence.

 **Pointer**

If it applies to you, create a section titled **NOMINATION(S)** where nominations for honors or awards can be listed. Even if you did not receive the honor or award, it is to your credit that you were nominated.

Writing Style

Just as there are conventional sections for resumes, there are conventional styles of writing a resume. Information is presented

- in reverse chronological order, and
- in phrases that begin with action verbs.

Look at Stephanie Student's resume for examples of this writing style.

Reverse Chronological Order

People tend to provide information in chronological order because we typically think that way when we recall events from the past. It helps us to remember more of the past when we review events in the order in which they occurred. Resume readers, on the other hand, want to first read about what you have done most recently, then what you did just before that, etc.

Phrases & Action Verbs

Descriptions of what you have accomplished are written on a resume in phrases rather than in complete sentences. Each phrase begins with an action verb. For example, someone who worked in a bicycle shop might write

"Assembled and repaired bicycles. Answered customer questions. Conducted weekly inventory of parts."

Some typical actions verbs used in resumes include

- organized
- coordinated
- developed
- created
- maintained
- taught
- prepared

61

- served
- conducted
- determined
- sold
- established

Use whatever verb describes the action required to complete the task. Avoid passive verbs like "did," "was," and "had."

Avoid using slang and insider terms that are not generally known. For example, the expression, "Did inventory" brings forth an image of the relatively passive activity of counting things, a necessary but often boring task. In the example above, the bicycle shop employee wrote, "Conducted weekly inventory of parts," thus making a different impression. Here the reader learns that taking inventory is an important function. It is done weekly and it is done to maintain bicycle parts necessary to service customers' bicycles in a timely manner.

 **Pointer**

Ask someone to proofread your resume for spelling and clarity of writing. Ask your proofreader if it is easy to read. If you have selected a fancy or unusual font, something other than standard, easy-to-read ones like

Arial and Times New Roman, the reader may have to work to decipher the letters. *Think about some of those formally printed announcements* (wedding invitations are among the worst offenders!) that slow down your reading and make you pause, squint and wonder whether that letter is an "s" or an "f" or a "t."

You Decide

Advice is sometimes given to make your resume stand out by using brightly colored and oddly shaped paper, anything but the standard white or beige 8.5" x 11" paper. Following this advice will make your resume stand out. Now think about the person who will be handling it. Do you think that person will be impressed or annoyed if an oddly shaped resume physically sticks out from the numerous 8.5" x 11" papers that are his or her responsibility to collect, store and read? Also, think about that feeling in your eyes when you read print on a brightly colored background. In some fields like art and graphics, displaying your talents through creative expression is desirable. What will be best for YOU, a standard or a "stand out" resume? You decide.

Printed on the next page is a worksheet to help you get started with your resume. Fill in the blanks using "Sections of the Resume" as your guide. Remember to use phrases that begin with action verbs and place information in reverse chronological order.

_____

_____

_____

_____

_____

OBJECTIVE

To obtain a [type of field work] position in_____

EDUCATION

_____   _____

_____   _____

RELEVANT COURSEWORK

_____   _____

_____   _____

RELATED EXPERIENCE

OTHER EXPERIENCE

COMMUNITY INVOLVEMENT

INTERESTS

REFERENCES

Furnished upon request.

References for [YOUR NAME]

_____(Name of Reference)
_____(Job Title)
_____(Place of Employment)
_____(Phone #)

_____(Name of Reference)
_____(Job Title)
_____(Place of Employment)
_____(Phone #)

_____(Name of Reference)
_____(Job Title)
_____(Place of Employment)
_____(Phone #)

_____(Name of Reference)
_____(Job Title)
_____(Place of Employment)
_____(Phone #)

THE PORTFOLIO

A portfolio is a collection of materials showcasing your accomplishments. Some people use them when applying for employment. You should use one when applying for field work, particularly if you are applying to an opportunity for which there is competition. Presenting a portfolio to a sponsor makes a good impression. A portfolio helps you stand out and gives you an edge over applicants who have not taken the time to create one.

Creating a Portfolio

You may think that creating a portfolio will be a great deal of work, or you may think you do not have material for a portfolio. Putting together a portfolio is not difficult. You probably already have several items you can use. It is now simply a matter of putting them together.

Items to consider for a portfolio include

- a copy of your resume
- a list of your references
- items you created like projects, writing samples, poetry or artwork
- letters of thanks or commendation
- certificates of honor and awards

- nominations for honors and awards—<u>Note</u>: Even if you were not the recipient of the honor or award, it is to your credit that you were nominated and it should be included.
- photographs
- newspaper photographs or articles that mention you

Let's take a look at Stephanie Student's resume and see what may be available for assembling her portfolio. Possible items include

- a project, paper or report completed during any of the *Relevant Coursework* listed on the resume
- a disc or hardcopy showing her work maintaining the House of Worship's Web pages
- materials or a photograph from her job as a computer camp counselor
- possibly an award or citation from the movie theater, perhaps for selling the most supersized orders
- possibly a ribbon for a successful finish in the annual Family Fun Run 5K Road Race fundraiser, or a photo or newspaper article mentioning her participation
- materials related to one or more of the activities listed under *Interests* on her resume.

It is likely that you have items similar to these. To assemble them into a portfolio, you will need some type of binder or a presentation book. Clear plastic page protectors are good for displaying each item. A table of contents and dividers with tabs keeps the contents organized and easy to locate, particularly when the portfolio contains more than a few items. For each item it is a good idea to write a caption identifying the item and explaining what it tells about you.

When selecting items, choose ones that

- reflect your interests and abilities related to the type of field work you seek or
- tell something about you as an individual.

Keep in mind that as a student you are not expected to have as much material for a portfolio as a person with professional experience. Five to ten is a realistic number of items in your "beginner's" portfolio. Keep in mind that you will be accumulating more experience and therefore more portfolio material in the future. As your career progresses, you will be able to add to the portfolio you start as a student, possibly including items developed during the field work you are seeking!

If you want more information, search libraries, bookstores and the Internet for materials that teach portfolio creation in clear, simple terms. Review them for ideas and to help you visualize your own portfolio. Also, guidance departments and career centers may provide portfolio assistance and have samples available for viewing.

Introducing your Portfolio during the Interview

Interviewing for field work will be discussed in Chapter 3. For students who have a portfolio or plan to create one, here are some examples of how Stephanie Student can introduce her portfolio during interviews.

When the conversation turns to computer skills, Stephanie will want to mention her experience with Web page design. She might say,

> "I wrote a paper on basic Web page design for my Web Design & Development class. I have it here in my portfolio. May I show it to you?"

In another example, the conversation may be about what Stephanie does in her spare time. She can refer to her community service and say something like,

"I received a ribbon for participating in the Family Fun Run 5K. I have it here in my portfolio. May I show it to you?"

The interviewer will want to see what Stephanie brought to the interview. As she hands her portfolio to the interviewer, she might say,

"There are some other items in here that you may be interested in looking at."

She could mention one or two of them.

CHAPTER 3

The Interview

Sponsors want to meet you. They want the chance to see how you present yourself and to learn more about what you want to accomplish. They also want to know what they will be required to do as your supervisor. It is through an interview that a sponsor will learn these things. However, the interview is not just for sponsors. An "inter-view" is a viewing between parties. This means the interview is also an opportunity for *you* to determine whether these are the people and this is the place where you want to complete your field work.

What the sponsor is looking for:

- a nice appearance
- on-time arrival
- confident behavior

- information about you
- information about your academic institution's field work program
- relevant questions asked by you

You can fulfill these sponsor expectations by preparing for the interview.

Appearance and Timing

Your appearance is the initial impression you make. Be well groomed and dress conservatively. Do not wear faddish or provocative clothing. Remove excess jewelry, especially jewelry from any non-traditional body piercing. Avoid unusual hairstyles and unnatural hair color. Most sponsors prefer a conservative appearance. Some sponsors require it when workplace issues demand professionalism, safety or freedom from distraction.

Arrive a few minutes early so you can compose yourself and not feel rushed. Let someone know you are there by giving your name and the name of the person with whom you have the interview. If you see informational material about the sponsor while you are waiting, read it. You may learn something new about the organization and it could help you ask relevant questions during the interview.

It is typical for people to make small talk in the beginning when walking into the interview room and getting settled. This type of chit-chat usually includes references to the weather, questions about whether you had difficulty finding your way to the interview, and other topics of general interest unrelated to the purpose of the interview. Small talk serves as an icebreaker for people who are meeting for the first time and allows the person conducting the interview to choose the time when talk of you and the field work should begin. You simply follow the interviewer's lead.

Confidence = Assertive Behavior

Consider for a moment the person who looks down or around during conversation, looks anywhere but into the eyes of the other person. Imagine this person shyly extending a hand or worse, not extending it at all when a handshake is expected. Further imagine this person mumbling or speaking so softly that hearing is difficult. This person displays a lack of self-confidence and gives the impression he or she will not be assertive in the workplace, thus requiring a great deal of supervision.

Sponsors value assertive students who work independently because they do not require a lot of time for supervision. Obviously students require attention some of the time, but if you give the impression that you will be "needy," the sponsor will look for another, more independent type of student.

Behaving assertively conveys a sense of confidence that sponsors like to see. Assertive behavior includes:

- shaking hands firmly
- making eye contact
- speaking clearly in a conversational tone of voice
- smiling pleasantly

Confidence is also expressed when you are able to tell the interviewer why you are interested in the site and what goals you would like to achieve. Finally, as a student you will be expected to have little knowledge and experience in the field, however, if you are able to bring to the workplace a particular skill, be sure to mention it!

Providing Information

The sponsor wants information about the field work program and about you. Be prepared to provide this information. If they exist, bring materials describing the field work program. Provide the name and phone number of a contact person.

Bring extra copies of your resume. If an extra one is needed, you will be in a position to offer it. This makes a positive impression that you thought ahead and came prepared. If you don't have a resume, see the resume-writing section in Chapter 2.

If you have a portfolio, bring it. If you don't have one, consider creating one by reading the portfolio-creation section in Chapter 2. That section will also tell you how to introduce one during the interview. Most people interviewing a student in a non-art field will not expect a portfolio. By presenting one you will stand out, a definite advantage when there is competition!

Consider the following information and advice from Mr. B, a newspaper editor and experienced supervisor of interns.

From the Field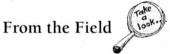

"One of the things I like to see in interns is that they can accurately represent what they can bring to the internship by showing me their abilities. A portfolio helps. A portfolio gives me a really good idea of what they've done, especially it if includes something that was actually used. That is very impressive."

Mr. B has this tip for inexperienced students.

> "If a student has no experience, my advice is to go to an event, like a ballgame, and write about it. Then bring your copy to the supervisor. This shows the number one thing I look for—motivation. I also want to know why the intern is interested in the field and why here at my newspaper."

Answering Questions

Be prepared to answer questions. Printed below are typical questions asked by sponsors. Advice on how to answer accompanies each one.

1) Why do you want to do your field work here? The sponsor wants to know why you have picked this site. Explain that the work done there is in your field of study or is of interest to you and that you want to learn more about it. Be specific.

2) What do you hope to get out of an experience here?
   The sponsor wants to know your goals. Describe two or three things that you want to learn or accomplish during your time there. Again, be specific.

3) What will I have to do as your supervisor?

Sponsors want to know the commitments required of them if they take in a student. For example, the supervisor may be asked to meet with you for a few minutes each day, or weekly for a longer period of time. Also, the supervisor may be required to verify your time sheets and complete an evaluation on your performance during the field work. There may be contact from someone at your academic institution in the form of phone calls and site visits.

4) Is there any compensation from the academic institution for supervising you?

Some institutions offer tuition reduction, credit vouchers or CEU's (continuing education units) to people who supervise its students. Some do not. Check with your field work advisor to find out if compensation is offered.

5) Tell me about yourself.

This "question" is an open-ended opportunity to share information about yourself. Interviewers like to hear about where you live and where you come from, your extracurricular activities, hobbies and special interests. They want to know what you are like as a person. This is also an opportunity to tell about any skills you have or distinctions you earned that relate to the site and your field work goals.

6) How can I get more information?

Some interviewers want to know who they can contact if questions or concerns arise. Be prepared to provide the name and phone number of a contact person. Typically that person will be the individual at your school, college or graduate school who administers the field work program or who will be overseeing you during the field work.

7) Does your school/college/graduate school have liability insurance?

Not many sponsors ask about the legal matter of liability in the event a student is injured on site. However, academic institutions typically carry liability insurance that covers their field work students. A copy of the insurance policy coverage page usually satisfies a sponsor seeking this information. Sometimes the sponsor's liability insurance covers field work students.

Asking Relevant Questions

Asking questions demonstrates your interest in the site, plus it is your opportunity to interview the sponsor, thus helping you decide whether it is the place you want to complete your field work. Consider asking some of these questions.

1) Ask questions about the business or agency to get a more complete picture of what goes on there.
2) Ask who will supervise you and what you will be allowed to do.

 **Pointer**

Some sites have confidentiality concerns that must be respected. However, if your exposure in the workplace will be restricted to menial tasks because of them, seek a different site.

3) Ask what time you will be expected to arrive and to leave each day.
4) Ask about their policy for reporting an absence due to illness.
5) Ask what type of clothing is appropriate.
6) Ask if the field work is paid or unpaid.

 **Pointer**

While co-operative education is typically a paid experience and service-learning is typically a volunteer experience, internships can be either paid or unpaid.

If you are seeking an internship, be sure to read the following section before you ask this question!

Paid vs. Unpaid Internships

The issue of paid vs. unpaid internships needs to be considered. While many companies offer paid internships, the internship program at an academic institution typically does not require payment. A problem arises when the employer desires your time be spent on tasks for which you are being paid rather than tasks that will expand your learning experience. For example, paperwork and clerical tasks are a part of most jobs. As such it is acceptable for interns to perform some clerical duties as long as activities with meaning are being performed and learning objectives are being accomplished.

Paid interns can find themselves in unfortunate situations like

- answering the phones and greeting people (because that is what they are being paid to do) instead of attending meetings where they could be learning more about the workplace and about group dynamics.
- entering data into a computer (because that is what they are being paid to do) instead of participating in a project that would allow

them to learn a process and to create a fin-
ished product (which, by the way, would be
a terrific portfolio piece!).
- filing and organizing office materials (because that is what they are being to do) instead of moving around the site to see how
different departments function and interface
with each other.

For the interns in these situations, earning, not
learning, is going on. They are not gaining meaningful experience, they are not acquiring valuable skills,
and they are not developing relevant resume or portfolio material. Further, these situations do little to
promote personal growth and self-confidence.

If you are interviewing with a sponsor of paid
internships, be sure to discuss what will be expected
of you *as a paid individual* and whether experiences
of substance in the workplace will be available to
you *as an intern*.

Closing the Interview

As the interview nears its end, ask when a decision will be made. You will likely have a deadline
with your academic institution and will need to
know your options before that time. It is helpful to
share this information with the sponsor. He or she

may ask you to call back for the decision. Find out when to call and then be sure to follow up in a timely fashion! If you do not call promptly, you will appear unreliable or uninterested.

 Pointer

Be Proactive

If the interviewer states he or she will call you, ask when to expect the call. If you do not hear by that date, call the interviewer. If you do not call, sponsors assume you are not interested. This is a technique used by some sponsors to make cuts from their applicant pools. However, it may also be a matter of the sponsor being preoccupied with the duties of the workplace and simply not having the chance to call you as promised. In the latter case, the sponsor will appreciate the reminder and you will be confirming your interest in the field work opportunity.

 Pointer

Committing to the Needs of the Sponsor

Some field work opportunities carry stipulations about time commitments that may exceed the time requirement set by your academic institution. A first reaction to this set of circumstances may be to assume it is not a good fit. However, this situation should be examined more closely.

If the opportunity is relevant, if the student is able to put in the extra time, and if the experience will advance the student by gaining skills, experience, resume material, and/or contacts in the field, it is highly recommended that the student consider making the commitment. It will be a win–win situation.

Field Work Savvy

CHAPTER 4

Accepting and Defining Field Work:
The Learning Contract & Goals

When you receive an offer from a site where you want to complete your field work, make a verbal commitment and fill out any paperwork required by the site. Your secondary school, college or graduate school may send to the sponsor a formal letter confirming the field work. Details like hours to be worked, goals to be reached and how your sponsor will provide supervision need to be discussed and agreed upon.

Details about the field work should be placed in writing in the form of a learning contract. Such a document is helpful in keeping all parties on track during your time in the field. It also serves as a kind of insurance policy for you in the unlikely event your sponsor is not providing the agreed upon supervision and experience in the workplace.

A learning contract is an agreement among the parties involved in the field work. In addition to you and the supervisor at the sponsoring site, there may be at least one other person representing your academic institution who will be a party to the learning contract. Your goals and duties, the amount and type of supervision provided, and any site visits by your field work advisor are some factors typically outlined in a learning contract.

A learning contract should contain basic information about you, about the field work site and about your secondary school, college or graduate school. Additional information may be required by your academic institution or by your field work sponsor.

The learning contract is not meant to be a rigidly binding agreement. It should be flexible to accommodate changes in goals that are not working out and to allow the addition of goals that were not discussed at the beginning of the field work.

Your Goals for Field Work

Setting goals in writing is a significant part of the learning contract. Without written goals, you run the risk of missing out on an in-depth learning experience in the workplace. You could end up performing menial tasks on the vague assumption that you will somehow acquire learning through osmosis. Don't let this happen to you!

Spend time considering what you want to get out of the field work and what learning goals are realistic for you in this particular site. Consult with your field work advisor who can provide guidance and suggestions for meaningful learning goals. Ask your supervisor for his or her professional perspective.

Developing goals with your supervisor creates a plan that is mutually agreeable. Plus, your supervisor's expertise is valuable for focusing goals on field-specific skills. Discussing goals is one way a supervisor serves as your mentor. Other ways will occur as you proceed through the field experience.

 **Pointer**

Provide your supervisor with a copy of "Tips for Field Work Supervisors" printed at the end of this chapter. Supervisors appreciate knowing what is expected of them and these tips provide ideas that will help them act as good mentors for you.

Effective Goal-Writing

When you know your goals for the field work, the next step is to put them into writing. A framework for developing each goal will be presented here, but first consider the elements of effective goal-writing: action verbs, measurable terms (terms that provide a "before and after" means of assessment), and a plan for achieving each goal.

Examples of action verbs include

- recognize
- diagnose
- evaluate
- compare and contrast
- determine
- conduct
- establish
- develop
- learn
- teach
- create

Below are three examples of well-written goals.

- My goal is to write a press release that will be used by a non-profit.
- My goal is to network a grouping of computers.

- My goal is to be able to develop a competitive estimate.

Here are some examples of goals that are too broad and too loosely defined.

- My goal is to find out as much as I possibly can about the business.
- My goal is to be a good worker.
- My goal is to show that I am the kind of person they want to hire by doing everything I am supposed to do.

These last three goals, while virtuous, are not helpful in defining what it is you will be doing during the field work. None of them use action verbs. All defy measurement (assessment) at the end of the field work. The first one is too general. The second one is expected of any student. The third one reflects a desire to be made a job offer. Future employment may be a motivator for the student, and it may even be something the sponsor is interested in considering, but it is not the purpose of field work and therefore is not an appropriate goal for the learning contract.

It is not enough to simply state your goal. You must develop a plan for how you will achieve that goal: What will you have to do? Who and what will help you? Common resources include your supervisor and other staff, a computer, professional publications, and any resources that are used to conduct business in the workplace. Finally, measurable terms allow the goal to be assessed at the end of the field work. A framework for developing effective goals is presented here.

A Framework for Developing Goals

Using the above three examples of well-written goals, notice how each one can be developed by using this simple framework.

Directions

Use an action verb to describe in measurable terms the goal you want to achieve, outline how you plan to reach that goal, and state how it will be determined when you have achieved the goal.

Field Work Goal # (sample)

[Student is in a service-learning position with a non-profit.]

GOAL
My goal is to write a press release that will be used by Community Health Services.

PLAN
I will become familiar with standard press release format. I will learn the background of the service being spotlighted. I will gather the details to be announced. I will determine the audience. I will review past press releases from Community Health Services. I will seek information and assistance from my supervisor and other staff.

ASSESSMENT
I will know that I have achieved my goal when Community Health Services uses a press release that I have written.

Field Work Goal # (sample)

[Student is in a co-operative education position with an information technology management firm.]

GOAL
My goal is to network a grouping of computers.

PLAN

I will read about computer networks. I will become familiar with procedures for networking computers. I will discuss with the users of the computers their needs for the linkage. I will observe my supervisor linking computers.

ASSESSMENT

I will know that I have achieved my goal when I am allowed to network a group of computers and the linkage is successful.

Field Work Goal # (sample)

[Student is in an internship position with a contractor to the construction industry.]

GOAL

My goal is to be able to develop a competitive estimate.

PLAN

I will review previous estimates by the contractor. I will observe my supervisor's handling of clients. I will determine an individual client's needs. I will consider the timing of the project. I will become familiar with costs and availability of labor and materials.

ASSESSMENT

I will know that I have achieved my goal when I have prepared an estimate that my supervisor says was calculated accurately and yields a competitive bid.

 **Pointer**

The length of the field work will determine the number of goals to be developed. Two or three goals can be achieved during a short-term field work while longer periods of field work allow time for more goals. If you have too many goals, you will not have enough time to accomplish all of them, plus the depth of your learning will be adversely affected. Too few goals will not utilize your time efficiently and you may feel unchallenged.

The Learning Contract

The learning contract is a tool that allows all the parties involved to establish a strategy for the field work prior to starting the experience. For the student, completing a contract helps determine opportunities for learning, defines ways to make meaningful contributions to the sponsoring site, and sets goals that will contribute to professional growth and development. For the sponsor, a contract defines the role of the mentor by outlining the amount and type of supervision, describing evaluations to be completed and scheduling site visits. For the field work advisor, the contract is a means for providing approval of the site, the strategy, and the amount of time required to receive academic credit or transcript notation.

The learning contract is also a tracking device that keeps everyone focused on the agreed upon strategy. The learning contract helps to keep the experience meaningful for the student and is useful for monitoring progress on goals.

A sample learning contract is printed here. Each academic institution and some sponsors will have their own versions of the learning contract. Use this sample as a place to record the basic data that will be needed when you complete a learning contract with your supervisor and field work advisor. Practice writing your goals in the blank goal-writing sections.

Field Work Learning Contract for

NAME OF YOUR SCHOOL, COLLEGE OR GRADUATE SCHOOL

Student Name

_____

Address during field work

_____

Phone

_____

Fax

_____

E-mail

_____

Name of Supervisor

_____

Title

_____

Name of Site

_____

Address

_____

Phone

_____

Fax

_____

E-mail
_____

Name of Field Work Advisor
_____

Title
_____

Address
_____

Phone
_____

Fax
_____

E-mail
_____

Defining the Field Work Experience

Describe the timeframe for the field work - start and end dates, days and hours you will be on-site.

_____

_____

_____

_____

Describe the sponsoring site, the type of work done there, and the department, division or office where you will complete the field work.

_____

_____

_____

_____

Describe the supervision you will receive. Who will assign duties, give instruction, provide feedback, and evaluate your performance? What will be the frequency of contact with your supervisor?

_____

_____

_____

_____

Describe your duties.

_____

_____

_____

_____

Describe how your performance during and after the field work will be evaluated. Will others besides your supervisor provide input? Will evaluations be written or verbal and how often will they occur?

_____

_____

_____

_____

Framework for Goal #__1__

Write out in measurable terms what it is you want to achieve (Goal), how you propose to reach it (Plan), and how it will be determined when you have achieved it (Assessment).

GOAL

_____

_____

_____

_____

PLAN

_____

_____

_____

_____

ASSESSMENT

_____

_____

_____

_____

Framework for Goal #__2__

Write out in measurable terms what it is you want to achieve (Goal), how you propose to reach it (Plan), and how it will be determined when you have achieved it (Assessment).

GOAL

_____

_____

_____

_____

PLAN

_____

_____

_____

_____

ASSESSMENT

_____

_____

_____

_____

Framework for Goal #__3__

Write out in measurable terms what it is you want to achieve (Goal), how you propose to reach it (Plan), and how it will be determined when you have achieved it (Assessment).

GOAL

_____

_____

_____

_____

PLAN

_____

_____

_____

_____

ASSESSMENT

_____

_____

_____

_____

Framework for Goal #__4__

Write out in measurable terms what it is you want to achieve (Goal), how you propose to reach it (Plan), and how it will be determined when you have achieved it (Assessment).

GOAL

_____

_____

_____

_____

Accepting and Defining Field Work:
The Learning Contract & Goals

PLAN

_____

_____

_____

_____

ASSESSMENT

_____

_____

_____

_____

Signatures of Agreement

I have developed this learning contract with the student and the field work advisor. I will provide the supervision described, meeting with the student regularly and completing evaluations on the student and the field work program. I will also be available for site visits. During the student's time here I will act as his/her mentor and make myself available to answer questions and to give advice and information about our worksite and about the field in which we operate.

_____   _____

Signature of Site Supervisor   Date

I have developed this learning contract with my site supervisor and field work advisor. I agree to meet with my supervisor and to perform the duties described. I will adhere to the expectations of the workplace in terms of procedures, dress, behavior and attendance. I will complete all academic and work related assignments. In addition to completing my learning goals, I will learn about and conduct myself in a manner consistent with the ethical and professional standards of the workplace and the field in which it operates.

_____   _____

Signature of Student   Date

I have been involved with the student and the site supervisor in the development of this learning contract. Fulfillment of this learning contract meets this institution's requirements for academic credit (or transcript notation). I agree to be available to respond to questions and concerns. I will conduct site visits on the dates noted and participate in the evaluation of the student and the field work program.

_____   _____

Signature of Field Work Advisor   Date

Tips for Field Work Supervisors from *Field Work Savvy* by Joan Milnes

Tip #1   Before the field work begins, plan to work with the student and the field work advisor from the academic institution to develop goals for the learning contract. Your knowledge of the field and the workings of your organization is a valuable resource for shaping appropriate goals for the student. Practical information about goal-writing can be found in Chapter 4 of *Field Work Savvy*.

Tip #2   Give your student meaningful work. All jobs include some tedious tasks and it is realistic for the student to perform some of them. However, true learning and the successful accomplishment of goals can only take place when the student is given substantive work.

Tip #3   Organize your student's workday. Develop at least a general plan. A structured schedule that includes projects, timelines, and check-in meetings with you is beneficial. Whatever the plan, develop it with the student and keep it flexible as needed during the course of the field work.

Tip #4   Help the student adjust to your work-place. Provide a suitable workspace and access to resources necessary to complete duties. Introduce the student to co-workers. Explain the expecta-tions of your workplace—proper at-tire, work hours, calling in sick, etc.

Tip #5   Be a mentor. Help the student under-stand your workplace as well as the field in which it operates. Be avail-able to provide feedback and answer questions. Ask for the student's opin-ion. Encourage the student to think *reflectively* about what is happening in the workplace and in the field. Chapter 5 of *Field Work Savvy* pro-vides a definition of *reflection* as well as strategies for using it during field work.

Tip #6   It is likely you have entered into a learning contract with the student and his or her academic institution. Review the learning contract with the student on a regular basis to track progress on goals and to identify any need to make changes.

Tip #7 Provide information as it relates to your student's academic studies. The student may be attending seminars designed by the academic institution to integrate classroom teaching with learning in the field. Ask for a copy of the syllabus or the outline of topics to be discussed. You can deepen the student's learning and understanding of the field by providing information, materials, and your professional perspective as they relate to those topics.

Tip #8 Stay in touch with the field work advisor at the academic institution. There may be site visits, letters and phone calls from the academic side, but feel confident about making your own contacts whenever you have questions or concerns. This will keep the field work running smoothly for you and for the student.

CHAPTER 5

Best Practices During Field Work:
Workplace Issues, Program Requirements & Reflection

In addition to actually completing the field work, you will benefit from an awareness of the best practices to be performed during your time in the field. This chapter discusses workplace issues of attendance, dress, behavior, and dealing with problems. This chapter also mentions various field work program requirements and it explains reflection. Reflection strategies to enhance your learning during and after the field work are also included.

WORKPLACE ISSUES

Committing to a field work opportunity means committing to the standards of your sponsor's workplace. It is your responsibility to adapt to the workplace environment. Each workplace will have its standards for attendance, dress, and behavior. Learn what they are and act accordingly. Here are some generally accepted and desirable standards, along with some examples of former students' experiences.

Attendance

Plan to arrive on time or a little early, and to leave on time or a little later. When you know you will be late or must be absent with illness, it is your responsibility to contact your supervisor.

For two reasons it is important to be reliable in your attendance.

- The sponsor will be expecting you to fulfill a certain role.
- You must complete the amount of time required by your academic institution to earn credit or transcript notation.

From the Field

As an assistant to the director of a traveling skit performed at schools to deliver a social message to young people, Anthony had landed a service-learning position that allowed him to use his theatrical and musical talents. The sponsor was completely accepting of Anthony's long hair, casual dress and laid back attitude. Unfortunately, his attitude grew too laid back.

Anthony began arriving late some days, and not showing up at all on other days. He never called to say he would be late or absent, and when questioned Anthony offered no explanation. His unreliable behavior became a problem for the acting troupe and the supervisor was compelled to contact Anthony's service-learning advisor.

Anthony remained elusive with his advisor about his erratic attendance. A reason could only be guessed. Personal problems? Substance abuse?

Because Anthony did not complete the time requirement for service-learning, his advisor was required to give him a grade of "F" or "incomplete." Had Anthony shared the reason for his attendance problem, his supervisor and advisor may have been able to work with him for a successful completion of his service-learning. He did not receive credit, a positive evaluation, or a letter of recommendation.

Dress

Plan to dress in the same manner as regular employees. If you have not been able to observe this before your field work begins, ask your supervisor about appropriate dress. If you forget to ask, or if you do not have a clear understanding, plan to wear something neat, but not jeans, and be sure to notice what people are wearing so you can dress appropriately for the remainder of your time there.

The advice given in Chapter 3 concerning appearance for the interview is repeated here because it applies to appearance during field work as well.

> Be well groomed and dress conservatively. Do not wear faddish or provocative clothing. Remove excess jewelry, especially jewelry located in any non-traditional body piercing. Avoid unusual hairstyles and unnatural hair colors. Most sponsors prefer a conservative appearance. Some sponsors require it when workplace circumstances demand professionalism, safety or freedom from distraction.

From the Field

Shelly was let go from her internship at a police station when she refused to remove the jewelry from her pierced eyebrow and nose. She accepted the personal risk involved, but the administrators at the police department were not willing to expose her

to the possibility of injury if a person in custody
became agitated and grabbed at her jewelry.

"I'm the one that would get hurt, and it was okay
with me. They made such a big deal about it!"

Shelly moved on to an internship with the dis-
patcher at a different police department.

"So I went to this other place that wasn't hung
up on the jewelry. It was kinda boring though just
being with dispatch."

Had she been willing to remover her jewelry for
a few hours on the days of her internship, Shelly
would have had a richer experience learning about
the operations of a police department at the first
site.

It is interesting to note that the second site which
allowed her to wear the jewelry kept her in a place
that was safe and out of view by most people.

Behavior

Show that you are interested in learning while
you are on-site. Ask questions, offer to perform various tasks, request that you attend meetings where
you might learn more about the site or the field.

From the Field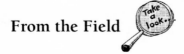

One experienced supervisor stresses that initiative is key during field work.

"There are times when no one can supervise the co-ops. My advice? They should offer to do something. Don't wait to be told!"

Also, remain alert and cheerful; stand and shake hands when you are introduced to someone; make eye contact and smile when you meet people. These behaviors will be well received by your supervisor and other employees. People are more likely to offer information and opportunities for learning to someone projecting an active interest than to someone who appears shy or intimidated. Remember, you are not expected to know everything there is to know about your worksite or the field in which it functions. Take advantage of your position as a field work student!

Behavior No No's

Every workplace has its own unique culture. The culture is influenced by the personalities of the employees and defined by personnel policies and sexual harassment laws. Rules of thumb for students include

- never participate in office politics or gossip
- maintain confidentiality about information you learn on site
- never make romantic overtures, not even in jest as this could be misunderstood
- aside from joining a group of employees for lunch, it is best to refrain from socializing outside of work during your time in the field
- immediately report to your field work advisor any unwanted attentions from an employee

Dealing with Problems

Problems occasionally arise during some students' field work. Most problems can be resolved by a simple discussion with your supervisor. In the unlikely event that talking with your supervisor does not alleviate the problem, then you should bring the matter to the attention of your field work advisor.

Try to not feel awkward about bringing a problem to your supervisor. The facts are that your supervisor wants to know, your supervisor will be pleased with your initiative to raise the concern, and your personal growth and self-confidence will increase.

From the Field

The director of a county youth services agency accepted Michelle for a service-learning position. The director assigned the office manager at one of the division's three locations to be Michelle's supervisor. The director visited this office one day each week.

Michelle soon discovered on the days of the director's absence that her supervisor would arrive late to work, make numerous personal phone calls, take long lunch breaks, and leave the office early. Also, the supervisor gave Michelle little work. The work she did assign was menial. Michelle told her supervisor she was able to do more work and that spending time with the judge and observing in the court room were especially interesting to her. When the supervisor did not respond to her request for more work, Michelle contacted her service-learning advisor.

The advisor encouraged Michelle to raise the issue with the director because she had accepted Michelle for field work and assigned the supervisor. Michelle was very uncomfortable with this idea, fearing her supervisor might be fired if she told the director what was happening. She preferred to leave the site and find a different service-learning opportunity.

Leaving a site without first making an effort to deal with a problem is inappropriate and unprofessional. To her credit, Michelle wanted to have a meaningful experience rather than follow her supervisor's example, and she wanted to stay with the county youth services agency.

Michelle successfully raised the issue with the director and expressed her sincere desire to not make trouble for the supervisor. The director was impressed with Michelle's courage and compassion. She was also grateful to learn where improvement was needed in the division for which she was responsible.

The director reassigned Michelle to a different field office with a supervisor who provided her with an appropriate service-learning experience. Michelle received a positive evaluation from her new supervisor and a letter of recommendation from the director of the county youth services agency.

PROGRAM REQUIREMENTS

Expect your academic institution to have requirements associated with its field work program. Requirements are based on age, skill, and level of
education. Here are some examples.

- A secondary school may require a brief Power
  Point presentation.
- Colleges may require essays or special reports.
- Graduate students may be required to con-
  duct research.

Other program requirements may include

- keeping a journal,
- logging your hours,
- attending meetings with your field work advisor and other students in the field.

Meetings may be held on campus or, if you are
completing field work a great distance from campus, e-meetings and Web based contact may be required. Consult with your field work advisor about
the program requirements at your high school, college or graduate school.

REFLECTION

A valuable learning tool commonly utilized in experiential education programs is a process called *reflection*. If you learn this process and practice it, reflection will become a source of enlightenment for you during field work and at any other time you choose, now and in the future.

The time you spend in the workplace is a learning experience about the field in general and about the sponsoring site in particular. However, learning from field work can be enhanced when strategies using reflection are employed. To utilize these strategies effectively, you must first become familiar with reflection.

What is Reflection?

Reflection simply means thinking intentionally. In your case it means thinking about experiences during your field work. When reflection is intentional and focused, new learning occurs.

Consider This

Sir Isaac Newton provides a good example of learning through reflection. Newton was the 17th Century English mathematician and physicist who discovered gravity after observing an apple fall from

a tree. Humorists prefer to say the apple hit Newton on the head, thus bringing to his attention the
gravity of the situation.

Sir Isaac followed the falling of the apple with
some intentional thinking about the fact that the
apple fell down, not up or in some other direction.
In other words, he *reflected* upon his observation.

Reflection = Intentional Thinking

Intentional thinking leads to discovery. This is not
to say you will always make historic, Newtonian
discoveries, but as a student, you will make discoveries about the world of work and about yourself.
Reflect and you will learn.

How to Use Reflection

Discussion and writing are two strategies that will enhance learning through reflection. Both are outlined below, but first, practice reflection. Begin by thinking about people and events at your field worksite in terms of

- what impresses you
- what surprises you
- what inspires you
- what is important to you
- why you felt happy/sad/proud/angry/confident/relieved/etc.
- how you would perform certain tasks
- how you would make decisions in the workplace
- how well the staff works together
- the tools used for motivation in the workplace
- leadership styles
- your assessment of the workplace culture

For example, you might think about your supervisor's leadership style. What is your opinion? Why do you think your supervisor acts this way? What would you do if you were the supervisor?

In another example, you might think about your feelings the first time you use on-site something learned in the classroom. How did you feel? Was the hands-on experience what you expected? Were you excited? Surprised? Disappointed?

During the act of reflection you may discover

- you learned something meaningful
- your reactions to similar situations in the future will be different
- you want to know more about a particular aspect of the workplace
- your thinking has changed
- you want to enroll in a certain course
- this is the job for you
- this is not the job for you

Now express your reflections verbally and in writing.

Talking about your Thoughts

A seminar or debriefing session with a field work advisor provides a verbal forum for the expression of reflection. Discussions involving other students allow you to compare experiences, ask questions of peers, share information, and learn from each other.

If your field work program does not include organized meetings, you could meet informally with
other students to compare notes, or ask someone to
be your sounding board. Ask a friend, your supervisor, a co-worker, a faculty person or advisor to
listen to your thoughts.

Writing about your Thoughts

Journals

Instead of a computer, use a notebook that you
can take with you to write anywhere, anytime. It is
not necessary to write in a journal every day. In fact
it may be best to not keep a daily journal. Daily entries have a tendency to become a chronological log
of what you did that day rather than a thoughtful
(reflective) piece of writing about your feelings and
opinions of your experiences during field work.

However, do write in your journal on a regular
basis. You could plan a structured series of entries,
every third day or every week, for example. Alter-
nately, you could plan to write at random intervals
as events that inspire you occur. If you choose the
latter, be alert to the passage of time. You do not
want to "forget" to write in your journal. Reflective
writing is most effective when it occurs soon after
the experience.

Essays

Some experiential education programs require essays about field work. A meaningful essay can be developed through reflection. For example, you might write an essay integrating the field experience with classroom learning. Discuss how you were able to apply something specific that you learned in the classroom to your duties in the field. Then discuss your feelings, opinions, impressions, etc. about the hands-on experience.

Pointer

A reflective essay or journal entry can be a suitable portfolio item.

CHAPTER 6

Closure, Evaluations & Letters of Recommendation

Just as there are issues to deal with when starting field work (issues like goals, what to wear, when to arrive, etc.), there are matters to be handled as field work nears completion. Closure, letters of recommendation and evaluations are relevant issues at this time.

Closure

It is important to bring closure to your field work, for yourself and for your sponsor. As the end of the field experience nears, you should remind the people with whom you have developed a relationship that you will soon be leaving. Give them the date. This will accomplish several things.

- It will help people who have been depending on you to complete certain tasks to begin thinking about alternate plans for getting those tasks done.

- If you have been working with business customers, they will appreciate knowing when to expect a change.
- If you have been working one-on-one with clients or with children, it will help them to prepare for change and to say good-bye to you.
- It will help you and your supervisor to focus on completing the goals in your learning contract.

Evaluations

It is very likely your field work program includes evaluations to be completed by your site supervisor. These evaluations seek feedback about your performance during the field work as well as feedback about the experiential education program at your school, college or graduate school.

It is also possible that you will be asked to complete evaluations about your supervisor, about your experience at the site, and about the experiential education program at your school, college or graduate school. Your feedback is helpful in several ways.

- It will be useful to future students considering your site for their field work.
- It will help your field work advisor determine the quality of your experience at the
  site and with your supervisor.
- It will provide an assessment of the experiential education program itself.

Your feedback is important. Plan to take the time
to provide honest and constructive information.

Letters of Recommendation

This is also the time to ask your supervisor, and
any other person who is in a position to do so, for a
letter of recommendation. It is a good idea to get
letters from people at your field work site. Letters
addressed "To Whom It May Concern" can be used
when applying for jobs, other field work opportunities, or further education.

However, do not assume people are willing to
write letters. Some people may feel they did not
observe you adequately to write about your performance. Others simply do not like to or want to write
such letters. Further, if your performance during
field work was less than satisfactory, you can expect people to say they cannot honestly write a favorable letter.

Unless it has been offered, the only way to find out if someone will write a letter is to ask that person. Near the end of your field work you will have a pretty good idea of who is willing and able to write you a favorable letter of recommendation.

CHAPTER 7

Best Practices Beyond Field Work

Your time as a student in the workplace has come to an end. What's next?

That's up to you. This chapter offers a few suggestions but first, and before too much time passes, write a thank you note!

Thank You Notes

Supervisors appreciate thank you notes from students. Be sure to send one to yours. Tell him or her you are grateful for the time spent working with you. Be specific about something(s) you learned or found especially interesting. If there were people besides your supervisor who helped you during field work, thank them, too. Thank you notes only need to be a few sentences long. Handwritten ones are the most personal.

Future Learning

Your field work may be ended, but your ability to learn from it can continue. Take what you have learned in the field and bring it into the classroom. You are now in a position to ask practical questions and to be the voice of experience during class discussions.

Some of you will receive and accept offers of employment with your field work sponsors. You will build on your field experiences as you continue working at the site.

Others of you will complete additional field work at other sites. You will be in an ideal situation to compare and contrast your experiences. Again, reflection can be a powerful learning tool.

Some of you have discovered through your field work that you do not want to continue in a particular field. You have learned an important lesson, one that could save you and your families much time and money. Consider yourselves enlightened and begin exploring other areas of interest.

Take the opportunity to continue learning through reflection. Write about your experiences in a personal journal or incorporate them into assignments in future courses. Talk about your experiences with people who share your interest in the field. Be an intentional thinker.

Pointer

Reflection is a lifelong habit of successful people in both their personal and professional lives. Those who make a habit of intentional learning are considered by others to be thoughtful, intelligent people. They are interesting and interested people.

Post Script

Congratulations! You have completed a field experience!

By participating in experiential education you have learned more than a few things about the workplace and about yourself.

- You have a better idea of what you want to do (or don't want to do) with your career.
- You made contact(s) in the field.
- You added valuable experience to your resume.
- You may have created a portfolio and added to it as a result of the field experience.
- You have had the opportunity to integrate academics into the workplace.

- You now have an advantage called *experience* over those who do not participate in field work.

Again, Congratulations! You have made "the organic connection between education and personal experience."

Notes

Notes

_____

_____

_____

_____

_____

_____

_____

_____

_____

_____

_____

_____

_____

_____

_____

_____

To order additional copies of

Have your credit card ready and call:

1-877-421-READ (7323)

or please visit our web site at
www.pleasantword.com

Also available at:
www.amazon.com
www.barnesandnoble.com
www.christianbooks.com

Printed in the United States
997800005B